T0064908

Jewish Wisdom for Daily Life

Sayings of Rabbi Menahem Mendl of Kotzk

Selected and edited by Miriam Chaikin
Translated and illustrated by Gabriel Lisowski

Arcade Publishing • New York

Arcade Publishing books may be purchased in bulk at special
discounts for sales promotion, corporate gifts, fund-raising, or
educational purposes. Special editions can also be created to
specifications. For details, contact the Special Sales Department,
Arcade Publishing, 307 West 36th Street, 11th Floor, New York, NY
10018 or arcade@skyhorsepublishing.com.

Arcade Publishing® is a registered trademark of Skyhorse Publishing,
Inc.®, a Delaware corporation.

Art editing: Michal Piekarski

Visit our website at www.arcadepub.com.

10 9 8 7 6 5 4 3 2 1

Library of Congress Cataloging-in-Publication Data is available on file.

ISBN: 978-1-62872-318-2

Printed in China

For my grandmother, Regina Morgenstern
GL

For my great niece, Josie Alexandra Pearl
MC

Contents

The Sayings

INTRODUCTION

The cities, towns, and villages of Europe were full of thriving Jewish communities before the advent of Hitler in the 1930s. Most Jews were religious, and most belonged to one of two main schools of Jewish thought, though there were also subgroups and splinters of one group or another.

One school, conservative, believed Jews ought to follow established Jewish law and to worship God with established prayer and by established custom. The other main school, known as Hasidim, which is Yiddish for "the Pious," believed God should be worshipped more spontaneously, with joy and with song and dance.

Although large communities of Jews settled in most European cities, Hasidim in Eastern Europe tended to establish themselves in shtetls, Yiddish for "little towns." These were self-contained communities, comprised of little wooden houses on unpaved streets, a main synagogue, smaller places of worship, a study house, schools, a court, a cemetery, and a busy marketplace. The head of the shtetl was a charismatic Hasidic rebbe, who was a *tzadik* or holy Jew, someone whom followers believed to have access to Heaven and whom they accepted as their undisputed leader—like a little king.

Such a Hasidic master was my maternal great-great-great grandfather, Rabbi Menahem Mendl (1787–1859) of Kotzk, in Poland. He was famous throughout Europe as a wise and strong-willed spiritual leader and was often called simply the Kotzker or Reb Mendl. People came from everywhere seeking his advice. The advice he gave was not always welcome, though. He was a stern and demanding leader. He minced no words and peppered his speech with insults.

Despite his reputation for rigor, young Jewish scholars came from far and wide to study with him. They had heard that the rebbe disdained the material world, ate little, and cared nothing for refinements of any kind. Even so, it is likely their first impression was one of surprise. Greeting them in the rebbe's study was not a neatly dressed man with a combed beard but a tall, thin man with a straggly beard, dressed in rags and wearing house slippers.

His reputation and appearance put no one off. The brightest and most committed remained to become his disciples. "His Hasidim," as he called them, revered him and strove to be like him, to the point of dressing in shabby clothes and replacing their shoes with house slippers. Their rebbe did not disappoint them. His scholarship and his reputation as a teacher led to the establishment of his own school of Hasidism. He was one of the great religious leaders who made of Poland a "Makom Torah," a place for masters in Torah to study.

Self-examination, truth, and the suppression of ego were central to the Kotzker's teaching. Some Hasidim in other cities and towns were opposed to him. The son of one rabbi, despite his father's opposition, went to study with the Kotzker. When he returned, his father asked him what he had learned in Kotzk. He said he had learned that it is possible for a person to become higher than an angel, if he wishes it, and that while God created the Beginning, that was only a start and it was up to the rest of us to carry on and build further.

Abraham Joshua Heschel, in his book *A Passion for the Truth*, finds similarities between the Kotzker and the Danish philosopher Soren Kirkegaard. Both advocated suppressing the ego, the love of self, which they believed led to corruption. To both, the inner life of a person was the main concern. Both sought to strip off

the outer garment of belief, the ritual acts, and to strive for truth.

Heschel also compares the rebbe to other Jewish thinkers. Vilna, in Lithuania, was once the center of Jewish learning. Rabbi Elijah, the Gaon (genius) of Vilna, was famous for his work correcting classical texts. While the Gaon was antagonistic to the Kotzker's Hasidic movement, the Kotzker had a high opinion of the Gaon and openly admired him. According to Heschel, "The Gaon attained tranquility through Torah study; the Kotzker delved into spheres where spiritual volcanoes erupt. His reward was restlessness and agitation."

The family name of my ancestor Reb Mendl, the Kotzker, was Morgenstern. He established the Kotzker dynasty, as such families were known. His eldest son, Rabbi David Morgenstern, succeeded him as the Kotzker rebbe and was in turn succeeded by other Morgensterns. The family kept the Kotzker rabbinate until the outbreak of World War II, when

Hitler's troops invaded Poland and marched across Europe.

Hitler turned the known world upside down in his quest for world domination. His forces rounded up and killed most Jews in work or death camps. Jewish families who managed to escape slaughter were uprooted and scattered to any port or place in the world that would take them in. Members of my immediate family sought refuge in Palestine, a British protectorate. My parents met there and there I was born, in Jerusalem, in 1946.

My father became Polish consul in Palestine until our family returned to Poland in 1948. Ten years later we moved to Vienna, where my father worked for the International Atomic Energy Agency.

Other members of our family remained behind, in Palestine, soon to be called Israel. My grandmother Regina was one of them. She made regular trips to Vienna to see us. As my Hasidic background always interested me,

I would question her about Menahem Mendl whenever she came. My questions continued by letter when she returned home.

She told about the Rebbe's fame and that he had always liked to be by himself, even when he was young. Later, when he became the Rebbe, he sought opportunities for solitude, to be rid of the mundane distractions that prevented him from basking in God's light. One day, no one knows why, he isolated himself from the people and remained so for the last twenty years of his life. There are conflicting stories about what drove him to this, but there are no clear answers. An air of mystery remains.

In my grandmother's mind, he did it to be rid of flatterers and the constant pleas of his people, so that he might better concentrate his thoughts on God's glory. He confined himself to one room of his house. The room had two doors. Hasidim still came to him to learn. The brightest, content to be in his shadow, assembled in an adjacent room. Through a slightly

open door he taught them Torah and Jewish texts. The second door led to the prayer room. When Hasidim came for religious service, he opened the door and from within joined his people in prayer.

Even in seclusion, during this period of separation, the Kotzker managed to conduct a private life, raising a family, marrying off his children to the sons and daughters of other Hasidic masters, and making himself available to other Hasidim to discuss communal matters.

In Hasidic circles it is said that each year, before the holiday of Passover, he burned the notes he used to teach. As a result, no written words of his remain. But his Hasidim salvaged what they could of his sayings and passed them on in writing and orally, and as the sayings circulated down the ages they came to be collected and quoted in books and articles.

My grandmother passed on to me many of them. My mother told me others. Our ancestor, the Kotzker, was a favorite subject of conversation in the family, and my uncle and brother and other relatives never tired of telling stories about him and repeating his sayings. Whenever I met someone who knew my family connection, I heard more stories, more sayings.

Here is a selection of sayings for which Rabbi Menahem Mendl Morgenstern of Kotzk became famous.

GABRIEL LISOWSKI

ABOUT HUMAN NATURE

A person often believes something
about himself that is not true.
Undeceive yourself. Know
who you really are.

I am I and you are you,
but if you try to be like me
there is no you, and
if I try to be like you
there is no me.

If you have problems, see if some flaw in yourself might be responsible. If you find no flaw— you are flawed.

A student once told me he did not involve himself with the community because he didn't want to take time away from Torah study. He was wrong. Our teachings tell us to offer help and benefit to the community.

Even the local dullard knows
something you don't.
Learn from him, from her,
learn from everyone.

If you hear your mouth say
you will do something, don't
believe it—until you see yourself
get up and start.

Don't chase around—here—
there—there—looking for
answers. Sit down. Ask yourself:
What is it I want?

Yes, hunger is a concern. But I am more worried about human cruelty.

It is true. There are temptations and corruptions in the path of wealth that are hard to resist.

Someone might commit an evil act, yet be a better person than you—kinder, more generous.

That scholar with his nose in
books, he learns and learns.
But does he know his wife
doesn't feel well? That
his child's heart is broken?

Just think—there is no one else like you. Cherish your specialness.

Whoever believes in miracles
is an imbecile. Whoever does not
is an atheist.

A leader who has fools for
followers soon becomes
a fool himself.

Only a monkey mimics the
behavior of his neighbor.

God made us—a remarkable
creation. How remarkable! We can
stay as we are, a finished person,
or improve ourselves.

Words are a clue to a person's
intentions. If he says, "I will,"
maybe he will and maybe he won't.
If he says, "I want,"
he is likely to be selfish.
If he says, "I am," pay attention
to what he has to tell.

Ignorance brings a person to grief.

There is nothing more whole
than a broken heart.

They hear but do not listen;
the words sit on their ears
but do not enter.

I do not value simple people
because they are simple.
They are capable of great mischief.
But when they have good hearts
and good habits—I do value them.

Some, when they do a good deed,
think they are doing God a favor.
What fools . . .

If you deceive yourself, you will never know the truth. Your beliefs will be tainted and your conclusions false.

Nothing grows by itself. You must plant it, feed it, care for it.

Be vigilant. The ego can sneak up on you and poison your motives.

Put a note in your pocket saying,
I am ashes and dust.
If you hear yourself bragging,
take out the note and read it.

Tears that haven't fallen are
the most bitter.

Mercy can be a sign of weakness.
I care more for justice.

Be alert, and be brief, even
when you pray.

A good friend may wish the best for you yet feel envy when some luck comes your way. It is momentary. He still loves you.

When it's not convenient to know
something, they close their ears
and pretend to be deaf.

Look at the power of a bribe:
A man never thought of giving
his wife a watch. But
offer him a watch as a bribe
and he can think of nothing else.

You don't like yourself? Maybe you have good reason.

Bury the lie deep, deep.
The truth will grow
in its place . . . and spread.

Because he likes herring, he is suspicious of anyone who is not a herring eater.

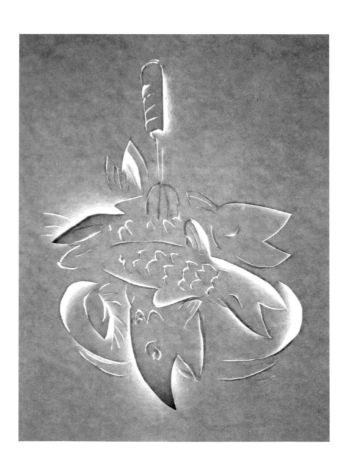

The mysteries of unknown worlds
are not your concern.

Busy yourself with trying
to unravel the confusions
in your soul.

Act when necessary, but know
when it's time to stop.

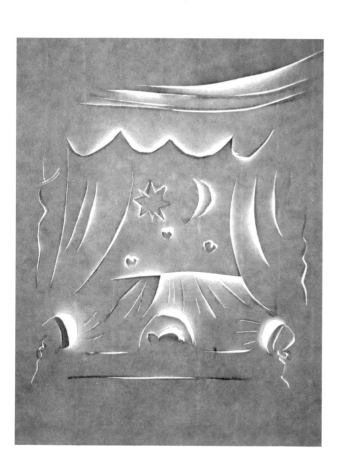

You have freedom of choice. If you
don't want to know something,
you can close your eye not to see
or your ear not to hear.

Know yourself, yes, but don't stop there. Repair yourself.

ABOUT LIFE

It's true what they say—I am hard
on my Hasidim. I shake them
into wakefulness. Gentleness does
not save souls.

Public opinion? I don't give a fig for it.

What makes for a successful
human relationship?
Treat everyone—especially those
who don't look like you or sound
like you—with respect.

Some teachers teach to make their students feel good. They give a massage, not a lesson. A teacher should do the opposite—upset students, wake them up.

Some say, If you can't go up,
go down, then go up. I say,
Go up even when you can't.

Be your own master!

Remember the phrase in Exodus,
"Keep far from a falsehood."
This is a prescription for a
good life, for being at peace
with yourself.

Love thy neighbor as yourself?
Never mind the neighbor.
Is your self worthy of your love?

We create nothing new.
All is within ourselves.
We must draw it out.

Everyone has something to
teach, even a thief:
if he fails, he tries again,
if he finds nothing of value,
he takes what he finds.

I say again—you have free will.
Use it to battle the traits
that spoil your life.

Study not to learn names and dates. Study the subject of goodness—learn what qualities lead to a good heart, to right behavior. Adopt them. Make them your own.

The donkey doesn't look back
to see how hard he has worked.
He is happy that now, unburdened,
he is free.

If you are in a superior position to another, let humanity pass between you, show a human face. Don't overdo it. God has enough angels.

When the noise stops, oh,
when the noise stops, how sweet
the sound of silence.

Don't tell me you don't sin because
it is forbidden. Tell me you don't
sin because you are too busy.

All that is thought need not
be said, all that is said need not
be written, all that is written
need not be published—
all that is published need
not be read.

We read, "When you go forth
to war against your enemies . . ."
This applies also to the enemy
within. Go forth to battle
your evil impulse.

If you think you are finished with self-improvement, you are indeed finished. You have closed all doors and windows of your being. Nothing new can enter.

In a big city, tall buildings hide
the face of Heaven.

Self-love leaves no room to love anyone else. Or even to be aware of anyone else.

A follower once asked me:
Reb Mendl, why don't you
write a book?

Who besides our own people will
buy my book? But they work long
hours and have no time to read.
Maybe, on a Sabbath, after
prayers, after a good meal and
songs of thanks, they might take
my book, stretch out on the sofa,
and open it to read.
But they would soon fall asleep.

Now tell me—why should I
write a book?

Why do I call him "a rabbi in a fur coat?" Look. He buys a coat. Who does he keep warm? Only himself. If he bought kindling, he would keep his entire congregation warm.

To eat, you must first catch the chicken.

Why fear death? You simply move
from this world into the world
of the Most High.

A promise is only so much
sound in the air—
until it is carried out.

It is not enough to learn
something. Do you understand it?

Take nothing for granted.
Corruption lurks in the halls of
justice and evil in places of succor.

If love and passion are not
controlled, they can bring
misfortune. Your heart has
no eyes to see with. Take
charge of your heart.

A person can perform endless
good deeds and still be a sinner.

A certain man asked me, How can you advise a businessman what to do when you are not in the business world? He didn't know that as an outsider I can see the picture more clearly.

He presents himself as a simple
person. It may be an act.

The ego—there is your villain.

You are not stuck with this impulse or that. You were given free will. Use it.

Be in awe of only one: God.
Fear only one: yourself.

Love is the bread and wine of life.

If you don't respect yourself,
no one will pay attention to you.
Why should they?

When things go well, choose a modest leader—when there are problems, a strong one.

The higher you rise, the longer
and more humiliating the fall.

Routine—doing the same thing
day after day—
can be a kind of jail.

It is all right to divide material goods—but never your beliefs.

If a religious act you perform gives
you pleasure, you are satisfying
your ego, not anything else.

I don't visit the graves of saints.
They are not there.

Freedom is a shaky business. And people are unreliable. Know where to put your trust.

Love is a hammer that can shatter
a stone heart into pieces.

It disgusts me to see them
acquiring and acquiring—another
hat, a second silk dress. We need
only one of a thing. Maybe two,
if it's shoes.

You have to keep trying.
If it comes easily, it is
not worth a yawn.

Some say, if you can't win,
give up. I say don't give up.
Someone has to win.
Let it be you.

You are troubled by alien thoughts? Which alien? What alien? Aren't they your own thoughts?

When you study, study deeply,
down to the roots.

People look up at Heaven and
wonder what happens there. They
should rather wonder what goes
on inside themselves—and learn
the truth of what they feel.

If heart and mind are not
in harmony, you cannot
master a subject.

He says he is depressed. Is he?
Or is he trying to escape his
responsibilities?

If you don't know your true self,
you will never fully understand
anything.

If a friendship contributes to your growth, keep it. If it does the opposite, drop it.

ABOUT THE SPIRITUAL

So what if I wear torn clothes and walk around in house shoes? What of them? Their silk jackets don't hide their big bellies. And their fur hats don't hide empty heads.

The ego separates a person
from God.

It is true: A *tzaddik** can issue a decree that God may fulfill. But make no mistake about it. God does not work for him.

*holy person

Angels are God's favorite creation. It's easy to see why. They are not jealous and they like to sing.

Why do I continually urge my
Hasidim to draw closer to God?
How else can one learn
God's ways?

To have faith you must forget your Self.

Walking with God on earth is worth more than all of life in the world to come.

I don't believe in blind obedience
to the Torah. Inquire, think,
gain understanding—
that is what must be done.

We read that God looked over His work and found it good. It was good as far as it went, but I see room for improvement.

People ask me: Reb Mendl, how do I draw closer to God? Don't they know God is everywhere?

Even on the darkest day, you can
find a corner of light.

A person can see more with
eyes of faith than with those
of the head.

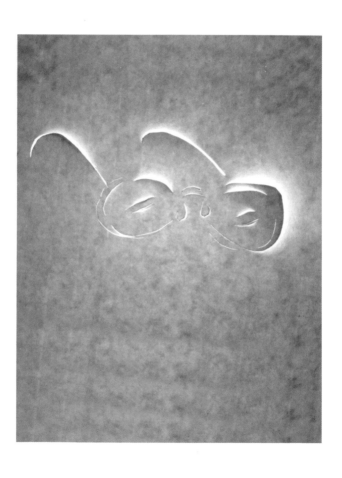

What does it mean—created
in the image of God?
It's not mysterious. A child
resembles a parent, and we
resemble God, who made us.

God made a good world for us.
We must make it better.

You are part of the community
and also a separate person.
Don't follow the crowd. Create
something new. God loves novelty.

Seek a purity of heart.

We read that at Sinai people were overcome with love for God. I wonder—did they still feel the same when they got back to their tents at night?

Try to keep your prayers fresh.
If you repeat the same words
again and again, they lose their
meaning—a prayer grows stale.

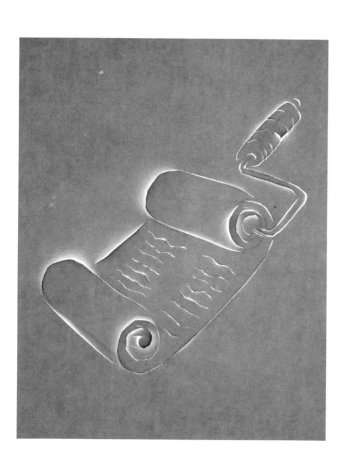

Truth is not what this one teaches, what that one says, or even what you yourself believe. Search for it.

When you have all you need yet
feel a lack, it is your soul longing
to be reunited with you.

People rob themselves when they
do not see the greatness of this
earth—where even a blade of grass
is filled with Divinity.

If we can see it, we think it must
be true. If we can't,
we think it doesn't exist.
The reverse is usually true.

They speak of the nearness
of God. God is not near.
But he is always there.

Who is wicked? An evildoer. Also a person who hates himself.

The individual is dear to me,
dearer than the community.

The mystics begin their discourse with stars and work down to the human condition. We start with the human condition and work up, toward Heaven.

Looking for God is like searching for a ring you lost in a haystack. You know it's there. You just have to keep looking.

Preparing for prayer is as valuable as prayer itself. The sages of old used to concentrate their thoughts on God first—to fill their hearts with love—then go in to pray.

A story: A man was singing songs
of praise to God when angel
Gabriel came and slapped his face.
Was it because Heaven did not
find him worthy? No, it was
because Heaven wondered if he
would still sing praises
after being slapped.

The psalmist says, "*Create in me a clean heart, O God, and put a new right spirit within me*" (51:10). I wish my followers desired the same for themselves.

If you accept the standards of
society, you will grow dizzy
with changing trends. But
God is One—one truth and
one standard for right and wrong.

A student asked me,
Where is the soul?
The Baal Shem Tov taught that
the soul is that part of God that is
in you. I say, just as you can't see
God, you can't locate the soul.

The most beautiful things cannot be seen—they can only be felt with the heart.

Some people say they have seen
angels. I myself have never
seen them, but I know for a fact
they are with me.

Believing is greater than seeing!

Human beings are God's alphabet.

I am sometimes asked:
What is the difference between
a Hasid and other Jews?
My people fear the Lord;
the others fear the letter
of the Law.

A person must work to make a living for the family. Hands should be busy with that. But the mind should be in Heaven.

What is faith? To choose Another over yourself.

God is playful.
He conceals and reveals himself—
and waits for you to find him.

I have no favorites—flowers, trees,
creatures that fly, that crawl—
everything in God's world
fills me with wonder.

It is too one-sided, this reliance on God's love and mercy. Know that God is also severe.

Isaiah (29:13) said two thousand years ago, in the name of God: *This people draw near with their mouth and honor me with their lips, while their hearts are far from me.*

Nothing has changed from that day to this. I say again: When you go to pray, leave your concerns and yourself outside—go in only with your heart.

I am not interested in unthinking followers.

They want to buy a horse or a pair of boots, so they ask their rabbis for help. *Shmendriks*.* Why don't they help themselves?

*Fools.

Wherever you let God in—there God can be found.

They claim their rabbis can perform wonders and miracles. It is entertainment for little minds.

Extremes. Utmost. To strain—
that's what I ask of my followers.
Only horses walk in the middle
of the road.

During a study session I asked my students: For what purpose was mankind created? Many answered, To purify the soul. They are wrong. We were put here to elevate the heavens.

If you need bread or wish for your wife to become pregnant, don't ask me to speak to God on your behalf. You don't need an intermediary. God hears everyone. Put the prayer before God yourself.

Stop a moment and listen to the rambling of a fool. That also is a form of charity.

They say I can raise the dead.
I don't know if I can.
I'm sure of one thing: I'd rather
raise up the living.

FOR FURTHER READING

—⁓—

And Nothing but the Truth according to the Rebbe of Kotzk. Translated and compiled by Rabbi Ephraim Oratz. New York: The Judaica Press. Inc., 1990.

Leaping Souls: Rabbi Menachem Mendel and the Spirit of Kotzk. Chaim Feinberg. Hoboken, New Jersey: KTAV Publishing House, 1993.

A Passion for Truth: Abraham Joshua Heschel. Sylvia Heschel. Woodstock, Vermont: Jewish Lights Publishing, 1995.
A study of Kierkegaard and the Kotzker rebbe and other Hasidic masters

Rabbi Menachem Mendel of Kotzk: A Biographical Study of the Chasidic Master. Dr. Joseph Fox. New York: Bash Publications, 1988.

The Sayings of Menahem Mendl of Kotsk. Simcha Raz. Translated by Edward Levin. Northvale, New Jersey: Jason Aronson Inc., 1995.